W9-APC-180

# THE GOLDEN GATE BRIDGE

BY
CAROLINE
ARNOLD

Franklin Watts
New York / London / Toronto / Sydney / 1986
A First Book

Cover photograph by Orville Andrews
Photographs courtesy of: Redwood Empire Association: pp. 8,
29, 33 (top), 34, 37, 44, 61, 67; Golden Gate Bridge, Highway
and Transportation District: pp. 19, 22, 23, 26, 30, 33 (bottom),
35, 38, 40, 46, 50, 53, 54, 58.

Library of Congress Cataloging-in-Publication Data

Arnold, Caroline.
The Golden Gate Bridge.

(A First book)
Includes index.
Summary: A history of San Francisco's famous structure, from
planning to the present, with a detailed description of its
engineering innovations and a list of facts and statistics about
what was once the longest suspension bridge in the world.
    1. Golden Gate Bridge (San Francisco, Calif.)—Juvenile
literature. 2. San Francisco (Calif.)—Buildings, structures, etc.
—Juvenile literature. [1. Golden Gate Bridge (San Francisco,
Calif.) 2. Bridges] I. Title.
TG25.S22A76  1986        624'.55'097946        86-11029
                ISBN 0-531-10213-0

# CONTENTS

# THE GOLDEN GATE BRIDGE

Acknowledgments

*Many people helped me in the
research for this book and I am grateful
for their time and expertise.*

*In particular, I would like to thank
Bruce Selby, Marketing Director, and
Robert David, Senior Graphic Designer,
Golden Gate Bridge,
Highway and Transportation District;
Stuart Nixon, General Manager,
and Norma Flanery, Publicity Director,
of the Redwood Empire Association;
and my parents, Les and Kay Scheaffer.*

# 1

# THE GOLDEN GATE

When it was completed in May 1937 and for twenty-seven years thereafter, the Golden Gate Bridge in San Francisco, California, was the longest suspension bridge in the world. A masterpiece of design and engineering, it was the culmination of the career of its builder, Joseph B. Strauss. Today, the Golden Gate Bridge continues to provide the essential link between the busy city of San Francisco on its south side and the suburban communities of Marin County to the north.

An average of 100,000 vehicles cross the bridge daily. Its majestic red-orange towers and elegant cables have become a symbol known round the world that stands for the city of San Francisco. More than one million tourists gather each year to take photographs of the bridge and to admire its beauty. According to the United States Chamber of Commerce, the Golden Gate Bridge is the number one man-made attraction in the United States.

The center span of the bridge rises *220* feet
(67 m) above high water, allowing room for
even the tallest ships to pass underneath.

The story of how the bridge was built is testimony to the hard work and determination of both Joseph Strauss and the citizens of San Francisco and North Bay Counties. They knew that such a bridge was the key to the development of the city and the communities to the north of it. Yet, even they did not dream how successful the bridge would become. In its first full year of operation, over 3.3 million vehicles crossed the bridge. Today, over ten times that many cars, trucks, and buses cross the bridge each year.

### What Is the Golden Gate?

The Golden Gate is a deep water channel that connects the Pacific Ocean and San Francisco Bay. At high tide the sea water rushes inward, through the Gate, past steep cliffs on either side. At low tide, it reverses direction and returns to the sea. Each second, over 2 million cubic feet (.056 cu m) of water flow through the 1-mile-wide (1.6 km) channel of the Golden Gate. The currents can be dangerous for ships, especially when the channel is hidden by fog. Yet, once through the channel, the water of San Francisco Bay provides an ideal, protected harbor for even the smallest sailing vessel.

The discovery of San Francisco Bay and its outlet to the sea came relatively late in America's history. When the English explorer Sir Francis Drake made his historic voyage up the coast of California in 1579, he sailed past the Golden Gate. To him it must have appeared as a mist-shrouded inlet, like so many others he had seen along the rugged northern California coastline. It was not until two hundred years later that the Golden Gate was discovered by Europeans.

In 1774, when Spanish explorers traveling north by land came to the east side of the bay, they climbed a small mountain called Grizzly Peak. From there they could see the opening of the Golden Gate and the Pacific beyond it. A year later, in 1775, the Spanish ship, *San Carlos*, was the first ship to come through the gate. For the next half century, the Golden Gate and surrounding area became part of the expanding Spanish settlement of California.

## The Formation of the Bay Area

Long before European explorers came to northern California, native Americans lived there, hunting and fishing along the shores of the Pacific and San Francisco Bay. They told a legend about what they believed was the creation of this outlet to the sea. According to this ancient story, what is now San Francisco Bay used to be a large fertile valley separated from the ocean by a steep mountain range. Inland from the valley there was supposed to have been a large lake. Each day the ancient Sun God would travel from east to west across the valley as he transported the sun across the sky. Sometimes the Sun God would stop on his journey to talk with the people who lived in the valley. One day, it is said, the Sun God met a beautiful princess and fell madly in love with her. The Sun God tried to steal her away, but as he ran away with her, he tripped and fell. According to the story, as he fell his toe knocked an opening between the valley and the inland lake and his arm made a gash in the mountain range between the valley and the ocean, thus allowing both the lake and ocean waters to pour into what is now San Francisco Bay.

Contrary to legend, modern geologists think that the Golden Gate used to be a deep gorge through which rivers from all over central California drained into the ocean. Over many thousands of years, the coastline gradually sank and the gorge became lower than sea level. As the ocean seeped inland, the valley eventually flooded to become a large bay. Today, the waters of San Francisco Bay are a mixture of salt water from the ocean and fresh water which has traveled from as far away as the Sierra Nevada mountains to the east.

The narrow entrance to San Francisco Bay was given its name in 1846 by an American writer and adventurer, John C. Fremont, who saw a similarity between it and the Golden Horn in Istanbul, Turkey. Fremont wrote, "To this Gate, I give the name *Chrysopylae*, or Golden Gate, for the same reasons that the harbor of Byzantium [now Istanbul] was named *Chrysoceras* or Golden Horn."

# 2

## A BRIDGE IS NEEDED

The city of San Francisco began as the tiny village of Yerba Buena, established by the Spanish in 1776 as a mission and military outpost. It remained a small isolated community until the 1840s. Then merchant ships began to dock there instead of at the California capital of Monterrey to the south, where they were required to pay heavy import duties. These merchants brought with them an influx of people and goods. In 1847 the community of Yerba Buena changed its name to San Francisco. By the end of 1849, San Francisco, once a village of less than 400 people, had grown to be a city with a population of 35,000.

### Crossing the Bay by Ferry

The need for bridges to join the peninsula of San Francisco with other communities on the bay became increasingly obvious as the city grew. Between 1848 when gold was discovered at Sutter's Mill in the foothills of the Sierra Nevada mountains to the east, and the outbreak of World War I in 1914, the population in the bay area had grown to 1,330,000 people. During that time the only way to cross the bay was by ferry.

The ferry companies prospered and grew, but as more and more people bought automobiles, the ferry system was pushed to its limits. In 1919, 123,000 automobiles were ferried across the bay; by 1928, that number had grown to over two million. On Labor Day weekend in 1930, the ferry line that ran from Sausalito in Marin County to San Francisco experienced its worst backup in history. On Monday, thousands of cars lined up at Sausalito to return to the city after the weekend holiday. The overcrowded ferry line got further and further behind until the waiting line— three cars wide—stretched back for over seven miles! Ferry line officials added more boats to the route, and finally got everyone across by 12:30 A.M. on Tuesday. Snarls like these helped consolidate public support for the Golden Gate Bridge project.

### A Bridge Is Proposed

The first public mention of the need for a bridge across the bay was published in August, 1869, in the Oakland *Daily News* by a man who proclaimed himself to be Norton I, Emperor of the United States and Protector of Mexico. Although the writer, a failed gold rush merchant whose real name was Joshua Norton, was not taken seriously, his dream was more prophetic than he knew.

Three years later, another man, railroad potentate Charles Crocker, again suggested a bridge. He wanted a means to bring railroad cars directly into the city of San Francisco. Crocker had his engineers prepare maps and estimates for a suspension bridge between Marin County and San Francisco. He presented his plans to the Marin County Board of Supervisors in 1872, but later abandoned them when it was discovered that he could more easily transport the railroad cars by steam ferry.

A bridge across the Golden Gate was not considered again for over forty years. Then, in 1916, James Wilkins, a newspaper reporter living in Marin County, who had attended the 1872 board meeting that discussed the possibility of a bridge, began an editorial campaign for a bridge across the Golden Gate. He promoted it both as a means of increasing business between San Francisco and adjacent communities, and as a source of civic pride. He wrote, "Even in the remotest times . . . the ancients understood the value of dignifying their harbors with impressive works. The Colossus of Rhodes and the Pharos [Lighthouse] of Alexandria were counted among the seven wonders of the world. The same tendency appears in our own times, witness the cyclopean statue at the entrance of New York Harbor [the Statue of Liberty]. But the bridge across the Golden Gate would dwarf and overshadow them all."

Wilkins was a visionary, and his articles influenced many citizens, including Michael M. O'Shaughnessy, the San Francisco city engineer. However, whenever O'Shaughnessy consulted other engineers about the feasibility of the project he was told that it was too difficult or too expensive. Then, in 1917, he mentioned the idea to a Chicago bridgemaker named Joseph Strauss, who had been hired to construct a series of small street bridges along the waterfront in San Francisco. Strauss was not only optimistic that a bridge across the Golden Gate could be built, but he also believed that it could be done far below the costs estimated by other engineers. Nonetheless, not much more was done about the bridge for a while. The city was involved in other projects and the country was still at war in Europe.

### The First Bridge Design

After the war ended Wilkins continued to press for a bridge in his newspaper columns and in November, 1918, the San Francisco Board of Supervisors asked Congress to authorize a federal survey of the Golden Gate channel as a first step in determining whether or not a bridge was feasible. After the survey was completed in 1920, O'Shaughnessy sent reports to three engineers—Joseph Strauss in Chicago; Francis C. McMath, president of the Canadian Bridge and Iron Company of Detroit; and Gustav Lindenthal, the man who engineered the 1,000-foot (304.8 m) Hell Gate Arch over New York's East River in 1916.

McMath never officially replied to O'Shaughnessy. Lindenthal's estimated cost of $56 million far exceeded the budget of $25–$30 million. Only Strauss proceeded with plans. Most engineers who saw Strauss's plan agreed that it accomplished what most people said could not be done. No one had previously built a suspension bridge as long as the distance across the Golden Gate. Most people thought that such a bridge would be too heavy. However, by extending either end of the support for the bridge toward the middle, Strauss had reduced this distance to a reasonable size.

Strauss's first design was a combination of a cantilever and a suspension bridge. A suspension bridge strings strong cables from two tall towers and then hangs the main deck of the bridge from vertical cables. A cantilever bridge usually has two vertical piers, and each supports a center arm and a matching side, or anchor arm, which counterbalances the center arm. Usually the two center arms meet, but in Strauss's plan they supported the suspension cables for the center span of the bridge. However, despite the plan and the growing enthusiasm of bridge proponents, many obstacles had yet to be overcome before the bridge could become a reality.

## Creation of the Bridge District

First the state legislature of California had to pass a bill to form a district that could collect taxes to provide funds to start the bridge; the district would also have the responsibility for building and maintaining the bridge. Such a bill was passed in May, 1923.

The United States Department of War had to give permission to build the bridge. It owned the land on either side of the Gate—the Presidio of San Francisco on one side and Fort Baker on the other—and it had the right to prohibit any construction in the bay which might affect shipping traffic or military logistics. After lengthy discussions and reports, the department's approval was granted on December 20, 1924.

In 1925 the bridge district began its campaign to organize the bay area counties into a tax district. In San Francisco County, which had the biggest population by far, many people felt that it was unfair that they would be providing most of the money for the bridge but would not have a proportionate share of control. Eventually, these problems were overcome, and in 1928 the Golden Gate Bridge and Highway District was incorporated, with six counties as members—San Francisco, Marin, Sonoma, Napa, Mendocino, and Del Norte. In 1929, Joseph Strauss was named chief engineer for the District.

# 3

# JOSEPH STRAUSS, BRIDGE BUILDER

Joseph Baermann Strauss was born on January 9, 1870, in Cincinnati, Ohio. Before Joseph was born, his father, a portrait painter, had emigrated to Cincinnati from Germany, and the family lived in an area of the city where there were many others of German heritage.

From their house the Strauss family could see across the great Ohio river which forms the border between Ohio and Kentucky at Cincinnati. Joining the two states was a huge suspension bridge over the river. This bridge had opened in 1866 and was known as "The Biggest Bridge in the World" with its 1,057 foot (322.2 m) center span. It had been built by the Roeblings, a famous father and son team whose other accomplishments had included the Brooklyn Bridge in New York. It is said by many that living in the shadow of this huge bridge was what influenced Strauss to become a bridge builder.

## Strauss's Early Life

As a boy, Joseph Strauss developed an interest in mathematics and science and when he was nineteen years old, he entered the University of Cincinnati as an engineering student. During the summers he worked as a surveyor for a railroad company, measuring canyons, rivers, and ravines where railroad bridges would later be built. His interest in bridges grew during his college years, and for his graduation paper he designed a bridge to go across the 50-mile wide (80 km) Bering Straits, connecting North America and Asia. Such a bridge has never been built, but if it were, it might well incorporate many of Joseph Strauss's ideas.

Strauss graduated from college as president of his class and as the class poet. Later, San Francisco writer Harold Gilliam wrote, "The two sides of his character, the imaginative and the practical, became the source of his genius. When the engineer in him warned that something could not be done, the poet challenged him to do it anyway. And usually the engineer found a way."

## The Bascule Bridges

After college Joseph Strauss worked at a number of jobs in small engineering companies. Then, in 1899, at the age of twenty-nine, he got a job with the well-known firm of Ralph Modjeski in Chi-

*Joseph Baermann Strauss,*
*designer and chief engineer*
*of the Golden Gate Bridge*

cago. At the time, a new type of bridge, called the bascule bridge, was becoming popular. This was a movable bridge similar to a drawbridge in which the roadbed could be raised to let tall ships pass below. A bascule bridge works something like a seesaw—one half of the deck is raised by lowering the other end with heavy weights.

The problem with building large bridges of this type was that the iron weights on the lower end were expensive. Strauss developed an alternative to this problem. He suggested making the counterweights out of inexpensive concrete. No one at the Modjeski firm believed Strauss's plan would work. Strauss was convinced that it would work, and because of this he left Modjeski to start his own engineering firm, Joseph B. Strauss and Company.

At first, orders were slow to come in to the new company. However, when Strauss finally did get a chance to build his own bascule bridge design, it was a success. Soon more orders came in, including one for the Elgin-Belvidere Railroad Bridge in Illinois, in which he had to sink one of the bridge supports into quicksand. This bridge remains a marvel of engineering even today. During his lifetime, Joseph Strauss built more than four hundred bridges including the Republican Bridge at Leningrad in the USSR; the Longview, Washington Bridge across the Columbia River; and the beautiful bascule span of the Arlington Memorial Bridge in Washington, D.C. However, most people will agree his crowning achievement was the Golden Gate Bridge in San Francisco.

## Redesigning the Bridge

Eleven years elapsed between the time the city engineer of San Francisco first suggested to Strauss the possibility of building a bridge across the Golden Gate and the establishment of the Golden Gate Bridge District. During that time Strauss continued to make refinements on his plan for a combination cantilever-suspension bridge. However, by 1929, technological advances in bridge-making had convinced Strauss to totally reconsider his original bridge design.

By then, new materials had made it possible to build a suspension bridge with a center span of more than 4,000 feet (1,392 m), the distance needed for the Golden Gate Bridge. This would make the cantilevers in Strauss's original design unnecessary. Also, research had shown that a rigid structure was not necessary to face the strong winds that swept through the Gate. In fact, a more flexible structure would be more able to endure high winds without stress. Thus Strauss and a junior partner in his firm, Clifford E. Paine, decided to redesign the bridge as a suspension bridge only.

In the new plan the main cables would reach from Lime Point on the Marin side of the channel to Fort Point on the San Francisco side. The bridge's center span would be 4,200 feet (1,280 m) long. At either end of the bridge a smaller trestle or trestle and arch bridge would connect the main bridge and the highway. Altogether, the series of bridges would be nearly 2 miles (3.2 km) long.

This new plan was far simpler than the first rather awkward design and its elegance promised to make it a monument of which everyone in the bay area would be proud. The blueprint for the new bridge was completed in the spring of 1930. The only remaining obstacles to building the bridge were financial.

### Raising Money to Build the Bridge

The Great Depression, which began with the Wall Street crash in October 1929, affected the bridge project in two ways. On the one

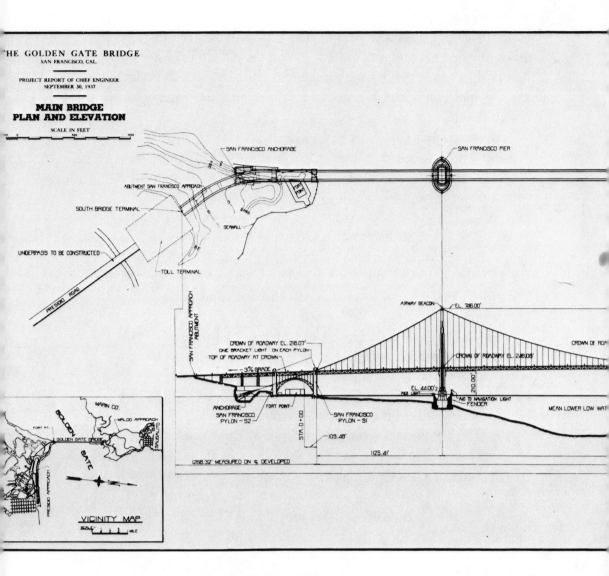

*Final plan for the Golden Gate Bridge*

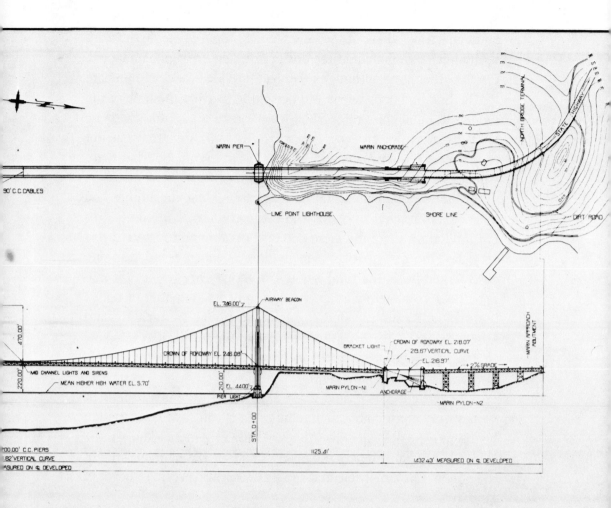

90' C.C. CABLES

MARIN PIER

LIME POINT LIGHTHOUSE

MARIN ANCHORAGE

SHORE LINE

NORTH BRIDGE TERMINAL

STATE HIGHWAY

DIRT ROAD

EL. 746.00' ⁊    AIRWAY BEACON

470.00'

CROWN OF ROADWAY EL. 246.08'

220.00'

MID CHANNEL LIGHTS AND SIRENS

MEAN HIGHER HIGH WATER EL. 5.70'

210.00'

EL. 44.00' ⁊

PIER LIGHT

STA. 0+00

BRACKET LIGHT

CROWN OF ROADWAY EL. 218.07'
219.67' VERTICAL CURVE

EL. 216.97'

+ 2% GRADE

MARIN APPROACH ABUTMENT

MARIN PYLON-N1

ANCHORAGE

MARIN PYLON-N2

⁊00.00' C.C. PIERS

1.82' VERTICAL CURVE

⁊ASURED ON ℄ DEVELOPED

1125.41'

1432.43' MEASURED ON ℄ DEVELOPED

hand, in a time when jobs were scarce, it promised employment to thousands of workers and for this reason had great public appeal. On the other hand, although taxes had provided money to prepare for the bridge, bonds needed to be sold to provide the bulk of the money to build the bridge. The plan was to repay the bonds by charging a toll for crossing the bridge. It was estimated that not only would the bonds be paid off within forty years, but that there would even be about $90 million in profits.

Strauss's original estimated cost of building the bridge had been $17.25 million. By 1925 the estimated cost had climbed to $21 million. In 1930, the increased cost of labor and materials had escalated the cost to over $27 million. Financing and planning costs would bring the total amount of money needed to $35 million. That year there was an election to decide whether or not to borrow the money needed to build the bridge by creating and selling bonds. The issue needed a two-thirds majority to pass. When the election was held in November 1930, the bond issue was passed overwhelmingly.

Nevertheless, at a time when most banks were investing their money very conservatively, finding a buyer for these construction bonds proved difficult. Eventually, Bank of America, under the leadership of San Francisco banker Amadeus P. Giannini, bought the bonds. This finally cleared the way for construction to begin in January 1933.

# 4
## BUILDING
## THE BRIDGE

The official ground-breaking ceremony for the bridge occurred February 26, 1933, on a clear cold day. An artillery salute began a parade which included dignitaries, enthusiastic citizens, and a group of engineering students from the University of California at Berkeley carrying an 80-foot-long (24.4 m) model of the bridge. After the governor of California, the mayor of San Francisco, and the bridge district president all spoke, and a telegram from President Herbert Hoover was read, people watched as a memorial plaque was installed, and a commemorative redwood tree was planted. However, the real excitement was that the actual construction of the bridge had already begun.

### The Piers

Before the bridge was designed, careful measurements had been made of the Golden Gate channel. They showed that the water

*Building the pier for
the south tower, December 1934*

reached a maximum depth of 250 feet (76.2 m) below the surface. On the north side, the channel dropped off sharply. Thus, the north pier would have to be built near shore. However, on the south side, the channel sloped gradually and allowed that pier to be built in the water. The channel was too wide for both piers to be built on shore.

The first part of the bridge to be built was the north pier. It would support one of the two towers from which the main cables of the bridge would be suspended. At the same time, construction of anchorage blocks that would hold the cables in place at each end also began.

The north pier was built in shallow water at the base of the cliffs of Lime Point in Marin County. One of the first steps was building a "cofferdam," a sort of fence that would surround the construction site and allow the water to be pumped out so that earth could be excavated as if the site were on dry land. The inside of the cofferdam measured 178 by 264 feet (54.2 by 80.5 m). After the excavation was complete trucks worked constantly to fill it with concrete. When the excavation was filled, workers continued to add concrete until the pier rose 44 feet (13.4 m) above the surface of the water. This massive concrete block measured 80 by 160 feet (24.3 by 48.7 m) at its base and was estimated to weigh 90 million pounds (33.6 million kg)! From the top of this sturdy base, large steel struts protruded. These would attach to the cable tower which would rise a further 700 feet (213.3 m) into the air.

The construction of the north pier was relatively simple compared to the problems that had to be overcome to build the south pier. Unlike the north pier, which was next to the shore, the south pier had to be built in water that was over 1,000 feet (305 m) from the nearest shore and had an average depth of 65 feet (19.8 m).

To transport equipment to the site easily, Strauss decided to build a long trestle bridge into the water. One foggy night, shortly after the trestle was finished, a huge freighter, unable to see the trestle in the dark, crashed into it and caused a great deal of damage. The trestle was then rebuilt, but again part of it was destroyed in a violent storm. After it was built a third time, work on the pier began.

Because the water was deep at the site of the pier, Strauss decided to have the men work inside a device called a "caisson" rather than a cofferdam. A caisson is an empty chamber which, when placed in the water, traps air so that people can work on the sea bottom without having to wear diving gear. (The principle of a caisson is demonstrated by submerging an empty glass, upside down, into a bowl of water so that it traps a bubble of air.) To protect the caisson from wind and waves, a 27-foot-thick (8.2 km) fence, called a "fender," was built as a wall between the work area and the waves. When it was finished the area enclosed by this fender was bigger than a football stadium!

The first night after the caisson was placed inside the fender, a fierce storm broke out. As the caisson, which was something like a huge floating teapot, tossed about inside the fender, it threatened to crash through the walls and destroy the fender. Strauss quickly gave orders to remove the caisson. A later decision was made that it would be safer to abandon the caisson and use the fender as a cofferdam.

At first, a device called a "tremie" was used to pump concrete below the surface of the water to build up the base of the pier. When it was 30 feet (9.14 m) under the surface, the water was pumped out of the fender and the rest of the pier was built under

*By early 1935 the north bridge tower was
completed and the south tower partially finished.
In the foreground rises the huge pier for the
trestle bridge connecting to the south shore.*

dry land conditions. When the south pier was finished, it was, like the north pier, 44 feet (13.4 m) above the water.

## The Towers

Each pier provided support for one of the tall towers that would hold up the cables. The two sides of each tower were joined by steel beams. Each tower was constructed of a network of steel units called cells, which were fastened to each other with rivets. Over 600,000 rivets were driven into each tower!

The cells within each tower were interconnected in a complicated honeycomb pattern. This gave the tower strength but it also made it extremely confusing for workers. They often got lost just in climbing from top to bottom. In an article Strauss wrote at the time he was working on the bridge, he gave an example of the kinds of directions one had to follow to go through the towers. "Enter shaft at sidewalk level and take elevator to Landing S3. Then go down ladder in Cell No. 29 to platform at elevation 486'4½" and through manhole to Cell No. 28, then up ladder to elevation 491'11" and through manhole to Cell No. 27, then down ladder to elevation 446'8½" and through manhole to Cell No. 22, then down ladder to elevation 323'11" and through manhole to Cell No. 14, and then through manhole to Cell No. 13."

*Looking across the Golden Gate channel toward the south bridge tower, September 1935*

Although the cables expand and contract with temperature and weight, they do not slide over the tops of the towers. Rather, the tower tops are pulled back and forth. Normally, when the temperature is 70 degrees Fahrenheit (21°C) and there is no load on the bridge other than its own weight, each tower bends toward the shore 6 inches (15.2 cm). If the temperature goes up 40 degrees and the bridge is fully loaded on the shore side, the tower can bend as much as 22 inches (55 cm). The towers can also move sideways. A wind load that would cause the center span to move 27 inches (67.5 cm) would cause the towers to move 12½ inches (31.75 cm). Each tower has a total load from the cables of 123 million pounds (45.8 million kg).

## The Cables

Although the finished cables appear to be single giant lengths of wire, they are actually made of 61 smaller strands pressed together into a cluster, 35 inches (87.5 cm) in diameter. Each of these smaller strands is a bundle that was formed from 452 even smaller cables. Each main cable has a maximum strength of 200 million pounds (74.6 million kg)!

*Top: walkways suspended between the towers provided workers with a safe platform while they constructed the cables.*
*Bottom: sixty-one strands, each containing 452 wires, were fastened together to make each main cable.*

The huge saddles on top of each bridge tower
clamp the main cables in place.

*Each cable strand is attached separately
to the anchorage block.*

Before any of the cables could be made, guidelines were suspended and a walkway constructed to make a working platform for the men on the bridge. Then, at each end of the bridge, machinery was set up to unreel the wire which would form the cables. The reels, or "traveling wheels," rolled along the guidelines carrying single strands of wire back and forth across the bridge. Each reel held a coil of wire 160,000 feet (55,680 m) long. By the time they were finished, 80,000 miles (128,000 km) of wire were needed to span the gate!

After the cables were formed and compressed, they were tightly wrapped in metal sheathing. Where they passed over the top of each tower, the cables were fastened in "saddles." Each saddle is like a huge iron fist, clamping the cable in place.

At both ends of the bridge, the cables are secured by huge concrete anchorage blocks. Embedded in the blocks are long metal bars with holes on the end. These are called eye-bars. Just before the cable reaches the anchorage block it is fastened with a steel band. This is called the "splay point." After the band, the cables are divided into 61 strands which splay out to be attached to the eyebars. The eyebars extend back into the concrete for about 130 feet (39.6 m) where they end in heavy steel girders.

## The Roadway

The whole floor structure of the bridge hangs from these strong main cables. At 50-foot (15.24 m) intervals, steel ropes hang down and attach to the supporting trusses. At each point of attachment there are four parts of rope, each about 2½ inches (6.25 cm) thick. The roadway and sidewalks hang there like a giant hammock between the two towers.

Huge girders hung from suspender cables
would support the road deck.

A safety net, erected during the construction
of the road deck, saved the lives of 19
workers. Later, they formed a club in
recognition of their "close calls."

Like a hammock, the roadway swings slightly in the wind. Usually the sway is not noticeable, although a 100-mile-an-hour (160 kph) wind would move it out 21 feet (6.4 m) at the center. The roadway also moves up and down with the temperature and load. In the most extreme conditions it might rise or fall up to 10 feet (3.04 m).

Before the bridge was built, the United States Department of War held an investigation concerning the bridge. They wanted to make sure that the bridge would be high enough to allow high-masted ships to enter the bay. They also wanted to make sure that if the bridge were destroyed in a war, it would not block the channel. During one of these hearings before the bridge was built, Strauss was explaining how the height of the bridge floor could vary by as much as 16 feet (4.9 m) above the water. At the time, one of the opposing lawyers accused him of trying to build a rubber bridge. In fact, it is this flexibility that is the strength of the bridge, for it allows it to bend rather than to break under stress.

From the beginning of the construction, safety precautions were stressed. In a unique effort to protect the lives of the bridge workers, a safety net was placed under the bridge as the roadway was being built. It extended 10 feet (3.04 m) out from either side and 10 feet (3.04 m) in front of the construction. This net, which was like nets that are used for circus performers, saved the lives of nineteen men who would otherwise have fallen to their deaths. Near the end of the project, in an unfortunate accident, a platform and twelve men fell into the net, ripping it apart. Only two of the men survived. They were rescued by nearby fishing boats that witnessed the accident and rushed to the rescue. Despite this incident, the Golden Gate Bridge has one of the best safety records of any bridge ever built.

*By October 1936, the road deck
was halfway completed.*

The floor system of the bridge was much easier to build than the towers. Inside the towers men had had to work in poorly lighted cramped conditions and rivets had to be transported by pneumatic tubes. Out in the open air, the rivets could be tossed directly to the workers. Work also progressed more quickly outside because the safety net helped to quiet fears of falling.

The steel structure that would support the roadway was finished on November 18, 1936. That day the headline in the San Francisco *Chronicle* read, "The Gap On The Golden Gate Will Be Closed Today." At 2:00 that afternoon, Joseph Strauss personally manned the derrick which swung the last connecting piece into place.

After the supports were laid down, the concrete of the roadway was poured. It was put down in patches in order to equalize the weight and stress over the entire bridge. A temporary railroad track laid down the center of the bridge helped bring materials and fresh cement to the workers.

Finally, on April 15, 1937, the paving of the bridge was finished. The total project had taken only four and a half months longer than originally estimated. Now, all that remained to be done before the opening was the clean-up.

# 5

## THE OPENING
## AND CELEBRATION
## OF THE BRIDGE

*The Bridge Is Finished*

On April 19, 1937, four days after the paving of the deck was finished, the first ceremony celebrating the completion of the bridge was held. Two companies of soldiers from nearby Fort Scott and a group of officials, which included Joseph Strauss and San Francisco's Mayor Angelo Rossi, marched to the center of the bridge. There, after listening to several speeches, they stood back to watch while a ceremonial gold rivet was driven into place by Edward Stanley, a bridge worker who had also driven the ceremonial first rivet. His nickname was Iron Horse Stanley.

Unlike the steel rivets for the bridge, which were always heated to make them pliable, the gold rivet, being made of a softer metal, was thought to be sufficiently pliable to be driven cold. However, much to the embarrassment of Stanley and everyone else, the gold rivet proved to be too difficult to drive, and after a great deal of effort, the attempt was abandoned. Later, the gold rivet was successfully placed in a nearby panel.

This first small ceremony marked the beginning of a fever of excitement that built toward the actual opening of the bridge six weeks later. There were two official opening days for the public— one on May 27 for pedestrians only, and one the following day for automobiles. Between May 27 and June 2 there was a gala celebration complete with parades, pageants, beauty queens and sports events. Guests were invited from as far north as Alaska and as far south as Guatemala, from eleven western states and from all of California's 58 counties. Delegations also came from numerous military and service organizations.

In preparation for the occasion, the bridge was lavishly decorated. Near the viewing area at either end, Girl and Boy Scouts planted blue lupins and golden poppies to represent the California state colors. On the bridge itself, thousands of feet of colored lights illuminated the towers and cables, making the bridge sparkle at night like a giant luminous jewel.

### People Walk Across the Bridge

The morning of May 27, 1937 was cold and foggy, but this did not deter the crowd of 18,000 people, all eager to be among the first to cross the bridge. Some, including a Boy Scout named Walter Kronenberg, had been waiting since 7:00 P.M. the night before. Kronenberg was identified as being the first in line to cross the bridge. Like the others, he had paid the required five cents pedestrian toll. Eagerly, he and the rest of the crowd waited for the barrier to go up.

Opening day for pedestrians, May *27, 1937*

At exactly 6:00 A.M., the foghorns at the center of the bridge blared, and the bridge was opened. Some people raced across the bridge, others walked sedately, and some just stood still and marveled at its beautiful structure. A few even spread out blankets for picnics on the bridge.

People were wildly exuberant about their new bridge and during the day many bridge "firsts" were established. Donald Bryant, a runner from San Francisco Junior College, was the first to sprint across the bridge. Two sisters were the first to roller-skate across. Among other record makers were the first baby in a stroller, the first priest, the first father and daughter to carry twenty-five pounds of Schuylkill County, Pennsylvania, coal across the bridge, the first person to walk all the way across with her tongue sticking out, the first dog, and the first person to cross the bridge on stilts. By the end of the day, nearly 200,000 people had crossed the bridge one way or another.

### People Drive Across the Bridge

The following day, May 28, 1937, was the official opening day for automobiles. In contrast to the day before, this was a much more sedate occasion. During the night, ceremonial barriers had been installed at various points across the bridge, each to be removed before the bridge would finally be open to traffic.

Beginning at 9:30 A.M. and proceeding from the Marin end of the bridge, the procession of cars moved slowly southward across the span. They stopped at the first barrier, a 16-foot-long (4.9 m) redwood log nearly 3 feet (.91 m) thick. At a signal, a group of log sawing champions competed to be the first to saw through the log. Two minutes and forty-seven seconds later, the contest was won

Cutting the ceremonial chain on opening day
for automobiles, May *28, 1937*

by a lumberjack from the state of Washington. The log was then removed, and the procession moved on.

The next barrier was a set of three chains, made of copper, silver, and gold, to be cut with an acetylene torch by dignitaries. The copper chain was cut first by Franklin Pierce Doyle; the silver chain was then cut by Mayor Rossi of San Francisco; and the third gold chain was cut by Bridge District Board President, William Filmer.

At the San Francisco end of the bridge, in front of the toll plaza, a line of beauty queens held hands to form the final barrier. Only after Joseph Strauss made a short speech in which he officially handed over the bridge to President Filmer did the beauty queens break their line. Thus ended a long, hard struggle for Joseph Strauss. The bridge that many had said couldn't be built was finally open.

At noon that day, in Washington, D.C., President Franklin Delano Roosevelt pressed a telegraph key announcing that the bridge was in public use. This was the signal for which everyone had been waiting. More than one hundred ships, ranging from mighty battleships to fleet destroyers and carrying between them more than 60,000 men, were waiting in the water below the bridge to begin their salute. Overhead, five hundred Navy airplanes flew in formation over the bridge and at the same time, throughout the bay area, every foghorn, ship's whistle, church bell, automobile horn and siren bleated, honked, and blared in a noisy cheer for the new bridge.

### The Celebration

One of the highlights of the week-long celebration that followed was a gala pageant performed on Crissy Field, just below the bridge. For this, a cast of three thousand costumed players, supported by a band of one hundred musicians, told the story of California and San Francisco from its earliest days to the present. It was presented on an enormous stage flanked by wings of towering redwood trees. The stage was faced by a grandstand that could hold 25,000 spectators. The backdrop to the stage was the bridge itself. A theme running through many episodes of the pageant was the great barrier formed by the Golden Gate, and its eventual conquest by the Golden Gate Bridge. Other events of the week included balls, fashion shows, swimming, wrestling, yacht races, nightly fireworks, a military parade, and children's races. It was the most elaborate celebration ever produced in the history of San Francisco.

Over the years, the bridge has witnessed numerous anniversary celebrations including the 25th, 40th and 45th anniversaries of its completion. On January 5, 1983, the fiftieth anniversary of the beginning of the bridge construction was celebrated. Several thousand people came to view an exhibit of historical photos, memorabilia, and contemporary children's art relating to bridge construction. Many of the men who had worked on the bridge came together again and shared memories. A garden plot commemorating the five year period of bridge construction was planted in nearby Golden Gate Park. Each celebration renews the public's fascination for this magnificent structure as well as its admiration for the courage and hard work of the bridge's designers and builders.

# 6

# MAINTAINING
# AND REPAIRING
# THE BRIDGE

Every year millions of tourists from all over the world photograph the beauty of the Golden Gate Bridge; every day, thousands of people cross it in cars, trucks and buses. Yet few of these people are aware of the enormous amount of work it takes to keep the bridge in good condition. Several hundred people, including engineers, painters, riggers, electricians, utility men, and laborers, work constantly to maintain the bridge.

*Inspecting the Bridge*

Inspectors are out on the bridge every day, carefully and methodically examining each part. Sometimes they check the main cables where they are fastened to steel bars in the huge anchorage blocks. Other times they may be testing the tension on the vertical cables. To check the supporting steel cables they must walk along the narrow path on top of each main cable. To get to the top of the

bridge to check the cable saddles, they must ride in service elevators inside the bridge towers. From the top of the elevator, they go through a series of steel chambers, up an iron ladder and out an overhead hatch to reach the outdoors. There, 746 feet (227.16 m) above the water, the massive cables are clamped tightly to the bridge towers.

Between 1967 and 1969 there was a major inspection of the bridge. It was discovered then that some of the suspender ropes and their connectors had corroded. As a result of the study, all the suspender ropes and their connectors were replaced between 1972 and 1976.

In another study, the bridge was tested to see if it could withstand the shock of a major earthquake. The tests showed that although the bridge would last through an earthquake that measured over eight on the Richter scale, several of the roads approaching the bridge needed strengthening. This was done in 1982.

### Painting the Bridge

Most of the people on the bridge service force are painters. Paint makes the bridge attractive and helps to protect it from the weather. Ever since it was finished in 1937, the bridge has been painted continually. The surface area of the bridge is approximately 10 million square feet (900,000 sq m) and it takes about four years of

*A safety inspector*
*checks the bridge.*

constant painting to cover it. Then, as soon as the job is finished, it is time to start all over again. The color of the bridge has always been a bright red-orange, known officially as "International Orange."

Many of the men who painted the bridge when it was first built continued to do so until they retired. In the early years they sat, suspended in bosun's chairs from wooden scaffolds and chiseled away the blistered remains of peeling paint by hand. Then they brushed on thick new coats of paint. Later, they stood on traveling steel scaffolds, sandblasting old paint with mechanized rigs, shooting on new coats of paint with pneumatic spray guns.

In 1984, the bridge painters began a project of sandblasting off the old paint and then applying an inorganic primer as a base before painting the traditional orange coat. The zinc undercoating will provide extra protection for twenty years or more.

### Electricity On the Bridge

Electricians are also important for the maintenance of the bridge. Eleven thousand volts of electricity flow into the bridge from a nearby utility station. At the bridge it is reduced by transformers into 2,300 volts. Electric power is essential for the functioning of many parts of the bridge, both inside and out. For instance, each time a motorist pays a toll, an electric machine records the transaction on a computer.

*Painting the bridge is a continual maintenance chore.*

Workers repair a beacon light on
top of one of the bridge towers.

Motorists must be able to see their way to and on the bridge, even at night or when heavy fog surrounds the Golden Gate. Electrically operated sodium vapor and mercury vapor lamps light both the bridge and its approaches every day between dusk and dawn. These kinds of lamps are particularly good for penetrating fog. Rotating beacon lights on top of the bridge towers guide airplanes through the Golden Gate, and lights under the center of the main span of the bridge show ships the way. All of these lights must be kept in good order by the electricians.

Electricians also maintain the foghorns on the bridge. Two of these, called "typhons," are on the south tower, just a few feet above the water. Their blare warns ships away from the tower when it is too dark to see. Two other foghorns, called "diaphones," help ships by showing them the way. These foghorns are in the middle of the bridge, directly over the channel used by ships going in and out of San Francisco Bay. Ship captains say that this is the only place in the world where they steer toward the sound of the foghorn instead of away from it.

## Keeping Traffic Moving

If there is an auto accident on the bridge, or a vehicle has engine trouble and must stop, a huge traffic jam can develop very quickly. The bridge tow service crew is always ready to remove a disabled or damaged vehicle from the bridge in order to keep traffic flowing smoothly. The tow service also provides emergency road service. It will help change a flat tire or will provide gas to a vehicle when necessary. When a truck carrying inflammable materials crosses the bridge, the tow service sometimes follows it with a fire truck. Sometimes the tow service picks up stray animals that wander onto the bridge or removes objects that have fallen from trucks. They do whatever is needed to keep traffic on the bridge safe and efficient.

During the entire time the bridge has been in operation, it has only been closed three times, all due to the weather. During a storm on December 1, 1951, winds through the Golden Gate reached 69 miles per hour (110 kph) and the bridge was closed for three hours. Afterward, a team of engineers checked the bridge thoroughly and declared it to still be sound. However, they recommended that additional bracing be installed on the bridge, and this was done in 1954.

The second time the bridge was closed was on December 22, 1982, when high winds caused the bridge to be closed for almost two hours. The bridge easily withstood the force of the winds. Earlier that year another storm had caused earthslides on the road approaching the bridge. Although the bridge was not closed there was almost no traffic on the bridge for three days.

On December 3, 1983, high winds caused the bridge to be closed for the longest period in history—three hours and twenty-seven minutes. During that time wind gusts reached 75 miles per hour (120 kph). There was no structural damage to the bridge.

### The New Road Deck

Since it opened in 1937, more than 100,000 vehicles crossing the bridge each day as well as nearly fifty years of wind, rain and fog have subjected the bridge roadway to severe stresses. Although regular maintenance work on the bridge is part of its routine care, it was clear by the mid-1970s that the roadway and sidewalks would need a major refurbishing. This would be both a costly and complicated task. It was estimated that the repairs would cost up to $50 million—more than the cost of the original bridge—and because there is no alternative route for the thousands of commuters who use the bridge each day, the bridge would have to stay open during the construction. There were five years of careful planning before any work began.

Fog rolls in from the ocean almost daily and envelops the bridge in salty mist. Over the years the salt had seeped through cracks in the concrete and corroded the metal supports in the sidewalks and roadbed. Since there was no way to repair this damage, it was decided that the sidewalks and roadbed would have to be removed. Section by section they would be ripped from their rivets and replaced with specially designed steel plates. The bridge was divided into 800 separate sections, each 15 by 50 feet (4.6 m by 15.2 m), and these would be worked on, one at a time.

On March 25, 1982, the actual repair of the Golden Gate Bridge roadbed began. First, trucks brought concrete barriers onto the bridge to separate the work area from traffic. To speed up the removal of the roadway, the rivets which held the concrete sections to the bridge had been cut out earlier and replaced with easily removable bolts. After the barriers were up, these bolts were taken out, and workmen began to cut the deck apart with diamond saws. Each piece was lifted by crane onto a truck and taken away. Then the new sections were brought to the site, laid in place, and quickly bolted to the bridge. In the course of refurbishing the whole bridge, it was estimated that 85,000 rivets were broken and that 250,000 bolts were tightened!

To minimize traffic congestion on the bridge during the construction period, it was decided that all work would be done at night when traffic was light. Four of the traffic lanes were closed

and worked on, while the remaining two stayed open. Work began at 8:00 each night and finished at 5:30 the following morning.

The new roadway is both lighter and sturdier than the original concrete and steel road. The old road had been constructed with reinforced concrete laid over 50-foot (15.2 m) long steel supports (called "stringers") riveted to the main bridge floor beams. Each 15 by 50 foot (4.6 by 15.2 m) section of the old road weighed about 44 tons (39.9 mt)! In contrast, the new road sections weigh only 26 tons (23.5 mt) each. They are made of steel plates resting on triangular steel pedestals which are bolted to the main floor beams. The surface is covered with an epoxy asphalt. Altogether the new bridge deck is 11,350 tons (10,295 mt) lighter than it was before refurbishing.

Materials for the new parts of the bridge came from all over the United States. For instance, the panels for the road surface were prefabricated in Utah, assembled in Napa County, and then brought to the Golden Gate. During the day, all the preparation for the nighttime work was done at a work area established near the north end of the bridge. Work conditions on the bridge were hampered by wind, noise, and traffic, so that doing as much as possible off the bridge made the project more efficient and safer. When the refurbishing was completed in the summer of 1985, it was estimated that it would help to extend the bridge's life by at least another one hundred years.

*Between 1982 and 1985 crews replaced the bridge deck, working at night to minimize traffic congestion.*

# 7

## CHANGES OVER THE YEARS

In 1938, less than a year after the Golden Gate Bridge was finished, Joseph Strauss died. In honor of his memory, a statue of him was built and placed near the toll plaza of the bridge. However, the most lasting memorial to Joseph Strauss is the bridge itself. Although its basic design has not been altered over the years, various small changes in its operation have helped improve its use to the community.

### *Tolls*

To help traffic flow smoothly over the bridge, a number of changes in bridge procedure have been instituted. In 1963, reversible lanes were begun. The center lanes could be used for either north or south traffic, depending on which was the heaviest. Removable lane dividers are placed in holes that separate the lanes, thus allowing the number of lanes going in any one direction to be flexible. Some have criticized this and said that it is confusing and turns the

Statue of Joseph Strauss

bridge into a giant cribbage board. Nevertheless, reversible lanes have greatly aided the flow of traffic on the bridge, especially during the heavy morning and evening commuter hours and also during weekend tourist periods.

In 1968, a system of one-way toll collection was begun. Thus, only traffic going into the city has to stop to pay. The drivers pay twice the one-way toll so that the same amount of money is collected with half the work and inconvenience. The Golden Gate Bridge was the first bridge in the world to try this experiment. It has been so successful that many other bridges around the world are now doing the same thing.

The last of the construction bonds that had been sold to finance the building of the bridge was paid off in 1971 with $35 million in principal and almost $39 million in interest having been paid. All the payments were financed by bridge tolls. Each vehicle crossing the bridge was required to stop at the toll plaza on the south side of the bridge and pay a toll.

At the time that the bridge was built, the public had been told by politicians that after the bonds were paid off, tolls would be abolished and crossing the bridge would be free. However, no one had anticipated how much the bridge traffic would grow. To help relieve the crowding, it was decided in 1971 that a toll would still be charged to bridge users, and that this money would be used to develop alternate sources of transportation. The toll money would also still be used for bridge operating and upkeep expenses.

### Buses and Ferries

As the number of cars, trucks, and buses crossing the bridge increased over the years, it became clear that one day the bridge would not be able to handle all the traffic. One alternative was to provide additional means of transit. Thus, in 1969, the California Legislature directed the Bridge District to develop a mass transportation program for the Golden Gate area. At this time the word "Transportation" was added to the District's title to show that it was now involved in the field of public transportation.

The first step toward providing mass transit occurred in 1970 when the District purchased a ferry to operate between Sausalito, in Marin County, and San Francisco. It bought and reconditioned a two-engine diesel-powered vessel called the M.V. *Point Loma*, which had originally been used as a tour vessel in San Diego, and renamed it the M.V. *Golden Gate*. This ferry has since carried over thirteen million passengers on its route between Sausalito and San Francisco.

In 1976 a second ferry service began operation between San Francisco and Larkspur, a centrally located community further to the north. One of the joys of traveling by ferry is standing on deck and feeling the salt spray in the wind or sitting inside and reading or eating on the way to work. Also, ferry riders do not have to worry about traffic or parking in the city.

When a severe storm in January 1982 caused floods and slides along the road approaching the Golden Gate Bridge from Marin, it prevented almost all traffic from reaching the bridge, thus making ferries the most convenient way to get to San Francisco. During this crisis three additional ferries were chartered from private companies by the Golden Gate Ferry Division, allowing them to expand their service, and on one day 12,275 passengers were transported. Normally, well over 2,000 passengers travel on any weekday. At the same time, the Sausalito ferry set a record of 4,118 passengers in one day. It normally carries over 1,500 a day.

In 1972, the District also started a bus service between Marin and Sonoma counties and San Francisco. The new bus service was an immediate success. Today, about 8,000 commuters are transported by it to and from San Francisco during the morning and evening commute hours.

Before the District began operating bus and ferry services, approximately 30,000 persons in nearly 20,000 vehicles were crossing the bridge each morning. Currently, the number of daily commuters is about 40,000 but, because many of them are using the mass transit system, the number of vehicles has grown only to 22,000.

## Toll Booths

To commuters, one of the most noticeable changes to the bridge over the years has been the toll booths. The original toll gates, which were designed by Joseph Strauss and architect Irving F. Morrow, had an Art Deco look that was typical of 1930s architecture. Lined up under a long canopy, they created a decorative gateway to the bridge. Each toll booth had rounded glass ends and openings on either side. It was placed between two lanes of traffic so that tolls could be collected either from the driver of a vehicle on one side or from the passenger on the other.

In 1962, a series of smaller, or "peanut," toll booths were placed between the original booths because single drivers had complained that it was too difficult to pay when the toll booth was on the passenger side. Another change came in 1968 when water-filled rubber "torpedos" were installed as crash pads in front of the booths. In 1970, a few automatic coin catchers were put in at the toll plaza, but they were unpopular and were soon removed.

The most radical change occurred in 1982 when all the toll booths were replaced by new, more comfortable and more efficient booths. The new booths make the collectors safer from high speed collisions, provide cleaner air for the employees, and make toll collecting faster and more accurate. They also allow traffic lanes to be wider than they were before, and provide more warmth for the toll collectors. The only part of the original toll plaza that remains today is the overhead canopy which protects toll payers and collectors from the rain.

Both the city of San Francisco and the Golden Gate Strait are often smothered in thick coastal fog. Marin County to the north is protected from much of this fog by high coastal mountains. To enhance its reputation as a gateway to sunshine, the entrances to the two tunnels that take the highway through the mountain on the north side of the Golden Gate Bridge were painted with colorful rainbows in 1971. Several small redwood trees and a sign were also installed to let travelers know what they would find as they continued northward.


*Billion Vehicles*

On February 22, 1985, a ceremony in the parking lot next to the toll plaza honored the symbolic billionth vehicle to be driven across the bridge. The car's driver, Dr. Arthur Molinari, a dentist who lives in Marin County and works in San Francisco, had been chosen as a typical bridge user.

Bridge officials do not know exactly when the one billionth crossing was made since only one direction is counted under the current procedures. The officials estimate that the actual billionth trip was made by an unknown motorist some time Tuesday, February 5. It is also impossible to compute Dr. Molinari's total toll. When the bridge opened it was fifty cents in each direction (with an extra five cents for cars carrying more than five passengers). In 1947 it went down to forty cents each way and later to a quarter each way. Currently, the toll is one dollar Sunday through Thursday and one dollar and twenty-five cents on Fridays and Saturdays. The toll is collected only coming into San Francisco.

Dr. Molinari is one of the bridge's oldest and best customers. He has been commuting to his office over the bridge since the day the bridge opened. He goes six days a week almost every week which means that he has made at least 28,000 trips over the bridge. His first trip was made in a 1932 Ford and his most recent in a 1974 BMW. At the ceremony, bridge officials presented Dr. Molinari with a case of champagne, a book about the bridge and a bridge worker's hard hat inscribed with his name.

Dr. Molinari estimates that he has spent five years of his life stuck in traffic jams. Nevertheless, Dr. Molinari has continued to love the Golden Gate Bridge. On the day of the ceremony he said, "The sight of it is as awe-inspiring as it was when I first drove across it on opening day in 1937. For it to be such a picture of grace and beauty is a miracle."

One of the other participants in the ceremony was 81-year-old William McCarthy. In 1937, he had been an aide to San Francisco Mayor Angelo Rossi and had driven with him in the first official car to go from San Francisco to Marin. McCarthy commented that, at the time the bridge opened, everybody thought the transportation problem over the Golden Gate Strait had been solved for all time. No one anticipated the enormous growth in traffic that would take place in the years ahead. At the present rate of 38

*The Golden Gate Bridge, looking toward*
*Marin County from San Francisco*

million vehicles a year, the second billionth vehicle will cross the bridge in the year 2001!

Until the Verrazano Narrows Bridge was built in 1964 to join Brooklyn and Staten Island in New York, the Golden Gate Bridge had the longest center span of any suspension bridge in the world. It is still one of the most beautiful bridges in the world. For half a century it has served as a critical link in a highway system that stretches the length of the west coast of the United States, joining the western states with Canada and Mexico. In the summer of 1937, as Joseph Strauss was leaving his job as chief engineer of the Golden Gate Bridge, he wrote: "No span of steel will tolerate . . . neglect. But if it is serviced by the generations who use it and is spared man-made hazards such as war, it should have life without end."

# BRIDGE FACTS

| Bridge | FEET | METERS |
|---|---|---|
| Total Length of Bridge (including approach structure) | 9,151 | 2,789 |
| Length of Suspended Structure | 6,450 | 1,966 |
| Length of Main Span | 4,200 | 1,280 |
| Width of Bridge | 90 | 27.4 |
| Width of Roadway Between Curbs | 60 | 18.3 |
| Clearance Above High Water | 220 | 67 |
| Deepest Foundation Below Low Water | 110 | 33.5 |

| Towers | FEET | METERS |
|---|---|---|
| Height Above Water | 746 | 227 |

| | | |
|---|---|---|
| Weight of Two Towers | 88,800,000 lb. | 39,960,000 kg. |
| Base Dimension (each leg) | 33 ft. × 54 ft. | 10.1m. × 16.5m. |
| Load on Tower from Cables | 123,000,000 lb. | 56,000,000 kg. |

*Cables*

| | | |
|---|---|---|
| Diameter of Cables Over Wrapping | 36⅜ in. | 0.92 m. |
| Length of One Cable | 7,650 ft. | 2,332 m. |
| Number of Wires in Each Cable | 27,572 | |
| Number of Strands in Each Cable | 61 | |
| Total Length of Wire Used | 80,000 miles | 129,000 km. |
| Weight of Cables, Suspenders and Accessories | 24,500 tons | 21,770 mt. |

# INDEX